How to

PROSPER

in

EVERYTHING

ERIC WILLIAM GILMOUR

SONSHIP

INTERNATIONAL

Copyright © 2017
by Eric William Gilmour

How To Prosper in Everything
by Eric William Gilmour

Printed in the United States of America

ISBN-13: 978-1727533293
ISBN-10: 1727533291

Bible quotations are taken from the New American Standard Bible (NASB). Copyright © 1960, 1962, 1963, 1968, 1971, 1972, 1973, 1975, 1977, 1995 by The Lockman Foundation.

Bible quotations marked (KJV) are taken from the King James Version. Public domain.

Bible quotations marked (BLB) is taken from the Berean Literal Bible, biblehub.com/blb.

Sonship International

*"Living in and by the sweet empowering Presence
of Jesus – seeking to bring the church into a deeper
experience of God's presence in their daily lives
and preaching the gospel throughout the world."*

www.sonship-international.org

facebook.com/ericgilmour
instagram/sonshipintl
twitter/sonshipintl
youtube.com/ewgilmour

SONSHIP INT'L
P.O. Box 196281
Winter Springs, Fl. 32719

Table of Contents

Foreword

In the almost twenty-three years that I have known Eric, I have seen him walk through many stages of life. Not just normal life experiences that most people go through. I've seen him walk through many stages in his life with Jesus. I am the woman God chose to be by his side and watch him discover these simple yet deeply needed truths that are 99 percent of the time overlooked or seen as insignificant. It hasn't been a walk in the park. One might think that being married to a man who is so in love with Jesus and obsessed with being alone with Him would be amazing. Like a fairy tale. I sit here chuckling because that is far from the truth.

It has been difficult. There are times I would be so angry standing in our bedroom staring at the closed closet door. I had this to do and that to do and I felt I was drowning in the responsibilities of life, alone. Don't misunderstand me. Eric is a wonderful father, very attentive to our daughters, who by the way adore him. He is an amazing husband and best friend to me. I just didn't always understand his need to be in there so much.

Oh if only I had just quieted my soul by obeying those gentle tugs I would feel in my heart to go away with Him myself. You see, the problem wasn't Eric being in his closet too much. The problem was letting the cares of this world trump His voice in my own life. But that is the beautiful thing about Eric. He obeys the voice of the Lord, always. He goes when the Lord says go. He doesn't ignore the pulling on the heart by the Holy Spirit. I wholeheartedly believe Eric was tailor-made for me because Eric is a walking example of a life wholly given over to Jesus and one who literally thrives in this crazy life by simple delight in God. And that has been the area in my own personal life where I have struggled.

It's a beautiful gift, marriage. He helps me in areas that I lack and I help him in areas he lacks. It hasn't always looked pretty, but we make a great team. Grateful just doesn't seem sufficient to describe what I feel towards God for allowing me the honor to walk this journey alongside Eric. He has given his life to the message that God birthed in his heart over the years.

So when you read this book, any of his books for that matter, know that the words you are reading are not just letters on a page. They are living words breathed into Eric's spirit from God Himself. He has waited and spent days upon days and hours upon hours alone with the Lord for years. I have witnessed it firsthand. The simple love and devotion Eric has for Jesus has forever changed me, and for that I am forever indebted.

I love you, babe.

— Brooke Gilmour

CHAPTER ONE

His Leaf Also
Shall Not Wither

"Only the enjoyment of Christ can keep us in right relationship with God."
— Witness Lee (*Life-Study of John*)

"A minister may be very faithful in his orthodoxy, most zealous in his service, and yet be so, chiefly, in the power of human wisdom and zeal. One of the signs of this is that there is little pleasure and perseverance in fellowship with Christ. Love of prayer is one of the marks of the Spirit."
— Andrew Murray

"God has waked my up in these last years to the extent that I feel like a new man...I worked oh so hard, and so much and asked God to bless my work. Now I try to pray more, get more blessing, and then let the blessing find its way through me to men. This is the better way...work less and pray more. That is what you need. I find fasting helpful for prayer."
— James Gilmour

_cↄ_

Psalm 1; Jeremiah 17:8 (KJV)

> "_Blessed is the man that walketh not in the
> counsel of the ungodly, nor standeth in the
> way of sinners, nor sitteth in the seat of the
> scornful. But his **delight** is in the law of
> the Lord; and in his law doth he meditate
> day and night. And he shall be like a tree
> planted by the rivers of water, that brin-
> geth forth his fruit in his season; **his leaf
> also shall not wither**; and whatsoever he
> doeth shall prosper. The ungodly are not
> so: but are like the chaff which the wind
> driveth away. Therefore the ungodly shall
> not stand in the judgment, nor sinners in
> the congregation of the righteous. For the
> Lord knoweth the way of the righteous: but
> the way of the ungodly shall perish._"

> "_Blessed is the man that trusteth in the
> Lord...For he shall be as a tree planted by
> the waters, and that spreadeth out her roots
> by the river, and shall not see when heat_

cometh, but her leaf shall be green; and shall not be careful in the year of drought, neither shall cease from yielding fruit."

Consistently floating to the surface in the midst of my conversations with men of God is the topic of a faithful life. Many great men who have gone before us, have been used in powerful exploits, and have preached the Gospel throughout the world, have fallen into tragic unfaithfulness in various areas. The church has witnessed the withering of their leaves and wondered how this could possibly happen.

Proverbs 7:26 states concerning the Spirit of Seduction,[1]

"she has cast down many wounded and many mighty men have been slain by her."

Notice the Scripture states, *"many,"* not few. Jesus used this same word in Matthew

---

[1] The name "Spirit of Seduction" is not actually in the Scriptures. I have named the influence this in accordance with its active pursuit of blinding men to God using enticing things. The Spirit of Seduction is personified in the Proverbs as a wayward woman but is not limited to sexual desires. The Spirit of Seduction is simply an enticement into a disobedience of any kind.

7:13 when He spoke of the broad way that leads to destruction,

*"**many** there be which go in…"*

Sadly, it is not an uncommon thing for men to start out right and end wrong. The withering of leaves, trees that are dried up and torn apart by life, is a reality that we cannot ignore.

It is also important to notice that Proverbs 7:26 records, *"**mighty** men."* It is not limited to the noticeably struggling and anemic Christian, but rather the one who may be seen as "**mighty** in the land." Remember when King David sang his song about Saul, who was anointed **mightily** and then became unfaithful to God through impatience, disobedience, and pride? David writes, *"Oh how the **mighty** have fallen"* (2 Samuel 1:27).

I am not trying to scare us into a vibrant life. I personally want to live my whole life never lacking the vitality of the Spirit of God. I know that you feel the same. I am convinced that the Lord is grieved by the lifelessness of many parts of His vineyard. His heart aches because of those who fail to produce fruit and wither away under the heat of this life.

CHAPTER TWO

Delight in God

"We cannot possibly be satisfied with anything less than – each day, each hour, each moment, in Christ, by the power of the Holy Spirit to walk with God."

— Andrew Murray

"The more we draw near to Him, the more we feel that He is so dear and lovable; the more we spend time with Him, the sweeter and happier we feel within."

— Witness Lee (*The Wonderful Christ*)

"The indwelling presence is the focal point of prayer. We need no wings, only a place of silence where we can center our gaze (upon Him)."

— St. Teresa of Avila

⤸

Don't we all desire to hear Jesus say to us at the end of our lives,

> *"...you were faithful..."*
> (Matthew 25:21)

Wow! Just the thought of the possibility of this moment is tear jerking. But if being found faithful is deeply desired amongst God's people, why is it so rare to find a man who lives a faithful life? Even Solomon in his day writes,

> *"A faithful man who can find?"*
> (Proverbs 20:6).

Is it possible to live our lives faithful to God? Is it possible to live our whole lives thriving with Divine Life? Yes, I believe it is, and I believe the key to spiritual vitality is found right here in the first chapter of the book of Psalms. Though many words surround this phrase and lead up to it, the answer is nonetheless found in this beautiful string of words, *"his leaf also shall not wither."*

Whose leaf will not wither?

The one who delights in the Lord.

What does that actually mean, "the one who *delights in the Lord*"?

It is simply the one who comes to God for satisfaction and consequently finds all his satisfaction in the person of God; the one who consistently comes to Christ for Life. Imagine a tree that is always green; no matter the weather or the season, it is always lively and flourishing. This is God's chosen imagery to convey to us what His desire is for all of us: a tree whose leaves are evergreen, unaffected by all the various seasons of this life.

I remember David Popovici saying to me, "Some men are walking revivals." Literally, some men live in a revived state. Isn't this God's desire for us all, to mount up on wings of eagles and fly above the storms of life and all this world's resistance against the Gospel?

God's purpose is that we would live in rich greenness, flourishing right in the face of the oppositions and tribulations of this world! Literally, that you and I would be filled with joy in trial and peace in turmoil. What is salvation if God hasn't given to us His Life that is greater than anything that can happen to us during the coarse of our lives? While everything crumbles around us, in the heat of trials and difficulties we can remain unaffected.

Oh dear reader, there is under His wings, a life that is incorruptible. There is Bread that always satisfies the soul. There is Wine that thrills without fail. There is a living water of life that is so glorious that even if we are put in prison, tortured, hated, or framed we are still thriving! Oh this wonderful Christ who has given Himself to us as the all-flourishing delight in God.

CHAPTER THREE

The Garden

"God made us for Himself that we might know Him, live with Him, and enjoy Him forever."
— A. W. Tozer (*Experiencing God*)

"Blissful experiences of Jesus are but a foretaste of what awaits us...Bridal love needs personal encounter with Him."
— Mother Basilsea Schlink

"The Spirit is none other than the fulfillment of the promise that God Himself would once again be present with His people."
— Gordon Fee

Do you recall God's original environment for His relationship with man? God made man and stuck him right in the center of the garden of Eden (Genesis 2:15). Let's look into this.

A garden is a place of life and produce.

The word "Eden" means "pleasure."

Isn't that incredible? The "garden of Eden" is the beautiful revelation of God's organic principle of *pleasure for Life and Life for produce*. Man was made to live in the delight of fellowship with God and from delight he was to be filled with Life that would enable him to exercise God's dominion in the earth.

Before and after the creation of man God expressed His desire for man to exercise His dominion in the earth (Genesis 1:26-28). Delight is crucial, because it is the only realm in which God intended His dominion to be expressed and exercised. In other words, delight in God

25

is God's only trusted platform for the expression of His rule. Without it something in the very foundations is amiss.

Delight is not merely some side issue of His presence, but rather the very means by which He imparts Life to us, and that Life frees us and empowers us to be able to obey Him. When God promised in Ezekiel 36:26-27,

> *"A new heart I will give you, and a new spirit will I put within you: and I will take away the stony heart out of your flesh. And I will put My Spirit within you, and cause you to walk in My statutes, and ye shall keep my judgments, and do them,"*

He promised to put right desires in us and cause us to walk in His ways. Kathy Walters once said, "He puts His desires in our hearts." Did you know that? He puts His desires in us so that walking in His will is delightful. That is the New Covenant.

Dear reader, God is speaking to you concerning His sharing of His very Life with you. That is the Glory of the New Covenant. We are partakers of the very Life of God. By this He receives glory. Glorifying God is dependent on fruit. Fruit is dependent on Life and Life is dependent on the enjoyment of fellowship. This is the glory of mutual satisfaction between God and man. The reconciliation is the restoration of God and man finding their pleasure in each other. Without this mutual satisfaction a man will not only lack fruit but he will also begin to lose Life and will little by little wither away.

Read this next sentence carefully. The unsatisfied heart is an idol factory. The unsatisfied heart fashions one thing after another to give its attention to. God is eclipsed in the heart that is not satisfied with Him. Anything can take His place. Even the things He has given to us. If we stare at anything long enough, it can turn into gold. If we fail to adore Him we will keep all the religious jargon and worship ourselves.

Today all kinds of things are sitting on the throne of men's hearts. We must realize that God will not share the throne of our hearts with a principle. He will not share the throne of our hearts with a theology or a gift of the Spirit. The throne in our hearts is made to be occupied by Him alone.

Man is not settled until Christ in our hearts is enthroned and unchallenged. Eden is teaching us that the pleasure of life is found in fellowship with His person. Enjoyment of God is the only platform upon which the exercising of His dominion and the pursuit of God is pure. Yes, enjoyment is the purest form of seeking God. And adoration is the highest form of enjoyment.

The Scriptures reveal that Adam's responsibility in this "garden of Eden" (this producing place of pleasure) was to *dress it and keep it* (Genesis 2:15). Literally to steward it, protect it, and guard it. It is obvious that stewarding pleasure would bring increase, but from what was the man to protect the garden?

The very command to keep the garden is evidence that opposition would come against our delight in God. What opposition came in an attempt to ruin the garden of delight? It was the thought patterns of the serpent. The unbelief and doubt inside of the snake's voice. We must guard against this. Dear reader, there will always be opposition to your delight in God. Cares of this world will come, the oppression of the enemy, trails, and difficulties will whisper in your ear. Protect your happiness and joy in His person.

What purpose does the enemy have in snuffing out our pleasure in God? After all, so what? Most Christians don't live a life of delight in God. It is important to note that our enemy knows that as long as man is dwelling in the place of pleasure, God Himself is our Life. God Himself causes increase and fruitfulness in our lives.

The enemy's attack on pleasure is really an attack on divine Life and therefore divine fruit. His attack is against the experience and enjoyment of our union with Christ. Ultimately, our fruitfulness and flourishing is an indication of enjoyment of our oneness with God. It is an outward sign that things are alive internally. Jesus said, *"My Father, abiding in me does His works"* (John 14:10). Works are to issue out of oneness with God and are an indication of union with God. Union with God is our Sonship. The means by which we experience our Sonship is through fellowship.

I must make a note here. There is something called "Christian Hedonism." The "Christian hedonist" seeks pleasure. The garden is pleasure, but not pleasure in and of itself. It is the pleasure of experiencing union with God through fellowship. Pleasure is not our focus; union is. But the means of union and the experience of our union is enjoyment.

In verse 10 of Genesis chapter 2 the Scripture records that in Eden (this Life of pleasure in God), *"a river went out of the garden."* This is the refreshing waters of the Spirit coming in and going out. In pleasure the river inside is able to flow out. The glory realm is not the force of discipline but the flow of delight. It is not a result of efforts but rest. If we will come to Him and cease our own activity, then His activity can truly begin.

In Isaiah 63 it is written, "He...carried them." He will lift us out of the treadmill of efforts by His own power. In the enjoyment of God His river flows and as we yield it will take us.

Inside the river the Scripture says, "*there is gold*." Gold! Here is where the things of value are found: in the river of the Spirit flowing in pleasure. The greatest things ever given to me from God were right there in the river of His presence, delighting in Him in sweetness and enjoyment. So it will be with you, because gold is in the river that flows in pleasure of His presence. This precious river is not a matter of rowing but flowing. As a matter of fact, oars are forbidden in the river of God. The NASB records Isaiah 33:21:

> "*...the Lord will be for us a place of rivers...*
> *on which no boat with oars will go...*"

We cannot put our trust in ourselves. He Himself is that river. If we will yield to the drifting of His person, then He may take us by His own power.

In verse 9 of Genesis 2 the Scripture says that, "*the Lord God made to grow.*" Man is not toiling, sweating, and striving; that is the curse (Genesis 3:19). Man's only job was to enjoy. This may upset people, but the means of stewardship is simply, enjoyment. The way to guard our delight in God is delighting in God.

A dear friend called me one day and asked, "What is one major evidence that a man is maturing in God?" I blurted out without even thinking, "Daily enjoying sweet fellowship with God." Could it be so simple? Yes. God has made it this way. The only thing that can produce godliness in us is Life from God. Life comes by the reception of Him who is Life. We received the Son and in Him have Life. Now we as sons are perpetual recipients of that same Life. This can only come about through the sweet enjoyment of exchange with God.

Back to our original text, the man whose "*leaf does not wither*" is that man who delights in God. Some may say, "But the Scripture says specifically, that 'his delight is in the law of the Lord,' not the Lord Himself." One quick read through Psalm 119 will convince us that the law, statutes, instructions, commands, and words of the Lord are all the means by which He is experienced and are themselves indicative of the Lord Himself.

David is not happy with ink and letters, but the Living God who satisfies the longings of his soul. But somehow, someway, through divine illumination he sees and hears God through the things written. He prays, "Lord, open my eyes to see the wonderful things in Your law." In Psalm 19:7-8 David points to the person of God experienced through the words of God:

> *"The law of the Lord is perfect, restoring the soul.*
>
> *The testimony of the Lord is sure, making wise the simple.*
>
> *The precepts of the Lord are right, rejoicing the heart.*
>
> *The commandment of the Lord is pure, enlightening the eyes."*

In essence he is saying, "I can see it, but I can't see it. There is more than just letters here. God Himself is with me through His words."

A few years back I had a very vivid vision in prayer that will give a picture to the point. I was in a dark room straining to read the Bible. It was fuzzy and very difficult to make out when all of a sudden a Light Being appeared a few feet away, and as I looked up at Him He drew closer and closer. As He did I was able to see clearer and clearer. Without His presence I was blinded, but when I became aware of His presence and turned my attention to His person, He became like a lamp for me to see His words.

What am I trying to say? It is imperative that the Scriptures themselves be cracked open by the weight of His presence. Then His voice can come out of them and into us and the transformation begins. For,

"In His Light we see light."

Once we come to the Lord and allow Him to be our satisfaction, which means we have given up on all other things and recognize that only He satisfies, this will inevitably produce in us an endless preoccupation with God Himself. David says, *"in His law does he meditate day and night."* This is a consuming, a literal obsession with the person of God. We learn from this that meditation is the irruption of delight in God and it reproduces the same. It is like a holy recycling.

David loves to blissfully muse upon God's person revealed to him through the Spirit opening his eyes to see the wonderful things in what has been written. Delight, pleasure, and enjoyment in God are evidence that God has captivated the heart. As my friend Daniel Kolenda would say, "If God has the heart, He has the man."

Though there are other things that are described in this psalm concerning the difference between the one who delights in God and the one who is not rapt in constant exchange with his God, we see that delight is easily the disintegration of self-rule. He who delights in God is a tree that is *"Planted."* God has rooted Him in the ground by His own river of Life.

The otherwise man is not planted at all. For the Scripture goes on to note concerning him that *"the wind driveth away."* He has no root but is uprooted and easily blown away. This is both now and in reference to the judgment. For our now greatly reflects what our end will be. And only if we are occupied with the eternal can we truly be of any significance in the now.

CHAPTER FOUR

Walk in the Counsel

"You and I individually must be in the place where we can say, "I have seen, and I know what God is after."

— T. Austin Sparks

"...knowing the depths of Jesus Christ is...a matter of being enveloped by God and possessed by Him."

— Madame Guyon
(*Short and Easy Method of Prayer*)

"For man it is more hurtful to himself if he seek not Jesus, than the whole world and all its adversaries."

— Thomas A. Kempis

ﮰ

Looking into the Spirit-breathed teaching of
David in this first psalm we learn more about
delight in God. He will not "*walk in the counsel
of the ungodly.*" What does this mean? The word
"walk" is used many times in the Scriptures to
point to the way we live. Here are just a few
examples.

Psalm 81:13: "*Israel would walk in My ways.*"

Galatians 5:16: "*…walk in the Spirit and
you will not gratify the desires of sinful
nature.*"

Ephesians 5:2: "*walk in love.*"

The enjoyment of God will cause us to
"*walk not in the counsel of the ungodly.*" Dear
reader, to live our lives in delight will preoc-
cupy our souls from ever listening to the
counsel of those who don't obey God. Listening
to His voice will deafen our ears to the whole
system of this world: its values, its mind-sets,

and its self-rule. Many of our problems are simply solved by the gentle turning our ear to His voice. Many of our problems are simply a result of not bending our ears to His sanctifying whisper of love.

I am reminded of Proverbs 19:27 in the New American Standard version:

"Cease listening…and you will stray."

If a man wants to slip away from God, he need only pay mild attention to Him. Hebrews 2:1 in the Berean Literal Bible (BLB) says,

"We must pay closer attention…so that we do not drift away."

In Psalm 81:11 the Scriptures show us what seems to be a repetition, but a closer look will reveal that attentiveness precedes obedience.

"My people did not listen to My voice and Israel did not obey Me."

"Listen" precedes obedience. If we do not listen to Him, we have no chance at ever obeying Him. We must take time to listen *for* Him before we will ever listen *to* Him. Some of us are so busy that we don't even think to listen for His voice. Here is the reason why so many of us lack the empowerment to obey. For obedience is when a man's life is yielded to the extent that God can perform through that man the things He has spoken to that man. Let me explain this further. In John chapter 12:50:

> *"I know that His commandment is eternal life; therefore the things I speak, I speak just as the Father has told Me."*

We're about to be let into the mind of the Messiah. Jesus is unveiling to us his own pattern of thinking, a revelation from which He Himself governs His life. His confidence is deeply rooted in this supernatural knowledge that is no doubt a result of being with His Father.

What is that governing knowledge that Christ had? It is simply that His Father's commandment, which means the things that He speaks, are eternal life. What does this mean? The things that God says have within them a life quality that is God Himself. Jesus does not say they were life or they will be life but that they are in this very moment a source of life that comes out of God and is God.

It is good for us to notice that God's voice must be Life to us, not only a command, meaning there is no option other than obedience, but also the recognition that when God says it, within His very words themselves is the life that God is. For the Life that God is, is also in the things that God says.

So what is this confidence? We do not need to strive, fight, wrestle, or make anything happen if we know that His commandment is life.

There is a wonderful aspect of God revealed in this passage. It is His Fatherhood nature that compels Him to open up His mouth and reveal to us His heart, His direction, and His wishes. Why do we hear His voice? We hear His voice because He is our Father. God only communicates with His own kind. This means that only by being born of Him are we recipients of Him.

CHAPTER FIVE

Stand in the Way

"Beware of thinking that the areas of your life where you have experienced victory in the past are now the least likely to cause you to stumble."

—Oswald Chambers

"Others may be content with being kept from what is visibly and grossly sin, but the obedient heart, seeks to walk with Him in unbroken communion."

—Jessie Pen-Lewis

"Refusing to sin is so far inferior to refusing to depart."

—Quote from the Author

The delighting one who stands in the presence of the Lord cannot simultaneously "*stand in the way of sinners.*" The "*way of sinners*" is the lifestyle of those who do not obey God. Sinners are those whose deeds issue out of self-rule. It is important to note that sins issue from sin. Sins are simply the fruit of a root issue, namely, the tyranny of self-rule (sin itself).

To delight in the person of God, captivated by His words, is what it looks like to no longer "*stand in the way of sinners.*" It means that delight in God will save us from conducting our lives in the same way that the wicked do: drifting in the destructive current of managing their own lives, without respect to the great King of kings. The sinners' craving for independence from God is their actual demise. Sin is independence. Death is independence from the Life of God.

CHAPTER SIX

Sitting in the Seat

"Meditation on the Scriptures eventually forms the ark of the covenant in the soul."

—John Cassian

"An unschooled man who knows how to meditate upon the Lord has learned far more than the man with the highest education who does not know how to meditate."

—Charles Stanley

"Meditation is the tongue of the soul and the language of our spirit; and our wandering thoughts in prayer are but the neglects of meditation; according as we neglect meditation, so are our prayers imperfect—meditation is the soul of prayer."

—Jeremy Taylor

Sitting in the counsel of the Lord will save us from the ruination of "*sitting in the seat of the scornful.*" What does this mean? Scorn is a very interesting word because it means contempt. A scornful person is someone who sees something as worthless. On the positive side, we scorn the world; we see it as worthless. On the negative, a scornful person sees God as worthless, unworthy of pursuit or consideration.

Oh but to enjoy the person of God is to be ecstatically blinded by the beatific vision of God Himself. You can tell what is worthless to a person by how forgotten it is. The things of great value stay ever and always before us. The scornful man knows nothing of the delightful meditation upon the person of God.

Oh David pictures for us his love for God when says that he will, "*meditate upon Thee in the night watches*" (Psalm 63:6). The "night watches" are special, not just the actual time of day when the sun has gone down or even the duration of "through the night," but also in those times in life when there is no vision, no sight, totally unable to see what may come, still will I fix my eyes upon You.

Here is the perfect place for my favorite quote from A. W. Tozer, "When the eyes of the soul looking out, meet the eyes of God looking in, there heaven has begun upon the earth" (*The Pursuit of God*). True maturity in God is delighting in God whether or not we ever receive the answers to our prayers.

CHAPTER SEVEN

Conclusion

"The man who has God for his treasure has all things in One. Many ordinary treasures may be denied him, or if he is allowed to have them, the enjoyment of them will be so tempered that they will never be necessary to his happiness. Or if he must see them go, one after one, he will scarcely feel a sense of loss, for having the Source of all things he has in One all satisfaction, all pleasure, all delight. Whatever he may lose he has actually lost nothing, for he now has it all in One, and he has it purely, legitimately and forever."

— A. W. Tozer
(*The Pursuit Of God*)

So if we put all three together we have the facts laid out. An endless preoccupation with God Himself through delightful exchange with Him will save us from the destruction of...

1. Listening to the patterns of thinking and value system of those who do not submit their lives to God.

2. Sinfully and shamefully managing our own lives.

3. Treating God with contempt.

God makes things very simple for us. You don't need to write these things down on a sheet of paper and check them off every day. God has shown us an easier way. It is as simple as "delighting in Him." The enjoyment of God is the divine and simple remedy for the patterns of thinking of this world. Delighting in God is the antidote to self-rule and it is the valuing of God above all.

CHAPTER EIGHT

So Simple

"The only work you are required to do now is to give your most intense attention to His still small voice within."

— Madame Guyon
(*Experiencing the Depths of Jesus Christ*)

"I have found it easy to obtain the presence of God. He desires to be more present to us than we desire to seek Him."

— Madame Guyon
(*Experiencing the Depths of Jesus Christ*)

"Every part of me that is not at rest is working against my internal sweet sensible experience of God."

— Quote by the Author

When anyone comes up to me and asks me for the secret to the truly spiritual life and a key to living a godly life, I instantly smile inside, simply because I know that even if I told them they would never believe that it is as simple as delighting in the Lord Himself. Enjoying God is the greatest power that there is. It keeps our leaf green and in the beginning passage from Isaiah it notes something very interesting, *"shall not see when heat cometh."* Isn't that great? The green leaf that is lively by the rivers of God's presence doesn't even recognize that the heat of life has turned up.

Oh how simple He has made it for us. It is not for the elite and robed in honor, but all, no matter how uneducated or lowly. No matter how rich or famous. It is as easy as breathing. But the sad fact that I have observed is that people would much rather hear about working their way into greatness through fasting or suffering or theological brilliance or some other thing they can work for. These things are all involved in the life of a son, no doubt. But the foundation for a son will always be his enjoyment of his Father.

Delight has a beautiful way of taking over our lives and somehow removes us out from underneath the influence of all the things that happen in this life. Delight will take us outside the mentally oppressive system of this world. It literally makes us strangers in this world in every respect. What a precious truth concerning the presence of God,

*"I am a stranger **with Thee.**"*

Not only is delight the realm of exercising God's rule, but delight is also the realm of God's rule in our hearts. Some may say, "I can't just delight in God all day. I have to work for Him as well." Dear friend, you fail to realize that delight is the reproduction ground for all God's works.

In Proverbs 8 Wisdom says that she performed all God's works followed by the statement,

"I was daily His delight."

God's works through Wisdom issue out of Wisdom's daily delight in Him. So it will be with each one of us. If we will listen to Wisdom, we will follow her same pattern: daily delight and the perfection of works. This may be harsh, but I believe it to be clearly revealed. Without delighting in the Lord there is no reception of His life. Without a reception of His life there is no fruitfulness. So we are left to work things out ourselves. Without life that comes through delight our works have the wrong source. Delight gives life, which is the springboard for effortless fruit.

Everyone knows the Scripture,

"Delight yourself in the Lord and He will give you the desire of your heart."

I want to say that this text is not pointing to us getting all the things we want in this life if we just delight in God, though He does give us richly all things to enjoy (1 Timothy 6:17). This text is not pointing to God placing good desires in our hearts as we delight in Him. Though there is probably some level of truth in both, I believe this verse is teaching us that in delighting in God, He Himself becomes the fulfillment of all our desires (Psalm 20:4). When these internal longings are filled with God, through delight in God, we are in the current of ease flowing contrary to all the patterns of selfishness and self-centeredness.

Oh dear reader, I can't tell you how many times I have watched people exhaust themselves and collapse under the weight of life simply because they, theologically or otherwise, left the Daily Cup of Sweet Wine from Heaven. Guard your delight in God. Keep it and steward it. How? Enjoy Him. Find the pleasure of His person every day and you'll receive more than strength far greater than any measure of resolve a human could employ: you will receive the Spirit of His desires.

Let me encourage you to be rapt in Him and preoccupied with His beauty. You will be blinded to all kinds of other things. For Mr. Competition, Mr. Comparison, Mr. Recognition, and Mr. Self-awareness are all assassins of your personal enjoyment of God.

The one who keeps his eyes upon the person of the Lord in delight is like "*a tree planted by rivers of water.*" He is firm. He is steady. He is planted. The "*rivers of water*" are a wonderful imagery of the presence of the Spirit. Jesus said in John 7:38 that "*rivers of living water*" would irrupt from the inside of us who believe.

Delight means being established in the presence of the Spirit. What follows is not a coincidence. The Scripture states that this one will "*bring forth his fruit in due season....*"

Fruitfulness springs out of the waters of Life. Produce comes from the stability that delight brings in our souls. If a man is not stable in God, he will never bear forth fruit. If "*a double-minded man is unstable in all his ways*," how much more will single-mindedness upon God stabilize our souls? Delight will stabilize our souls. Enjoyment will deliver us from the turbulence of competition, comparison, antsy activity, tiresome toil, and all kinds of other life-sucking things.

In my travels I meet all kinds of members of the body of Christ and it is sad to see that many are so antsy. They cannot sit still. Being antsy is an indication that we are out of rhythm with God. God is always sitting. He is always at rest. When we come to Him, He gives us rest (Matthew 11:28).

So many Christians are fighting to be recognized. They want to be noticed. They are dropping hints of their accomplishments. They are literally trying to build honor for themselves in the minds of others, all in an attempt to be "significant" or "relevant." Men are secretly seeking to carve out a celebrity-like distinction for themselves. All of these kinds of things are indications of lack of rest, the lack of a rest that only comes from the enjoyment of God. We must rest upon Him. We must still our hearts. The psalmist also writes,

> *"Stand in awe and sin not. Commune with your own heart upon your bed and be still."*

Stillness is the antithesis to sin. Living an antsy life is a sure way to live without root in God. So many of us are latching on to this minister or that missionary for an image of Christ and they soon end up trying to speak like them, adopting their language and mannerisms. These are all indications that God Himself is not being enjoyed. It is an indication that the person of Christ is not the focal point.

The danger with the intimacy movement is that many have merely adopted the language of it. Many only have the vocabulary of intimacy, not so much a personal intimate experience. All of this is a lack of rest that is indicative of no real delight in God. But if we want eternal fruit that is significant to God, then we must come to Him, delight in Him, and our enjoyment of Him will make everything else irrelevant to us simply because we will know by experience that He is inexhaustibly the satisfaction of our souls.

In Proverbs 9 Lady Wisdom cries out to the naïve and basically says, "Turn in here, I have a whole feast set up for you. Eat my food and drink my wine, that you may have life and revelation." This shows us that the protection from waywardness is eating and drinking at the Lord's table, the reception of life that delight brings.

In Proverbs 5 the Seductive Spirit is rendered powerless by simply listening to the Words of the Father's mouth (vs. 1,7). If we will give ourselves to the passivity of listening we will find the ease of God's Life. Many of us are so scattered, busy, and antsy that the passivity of listening is deemed all but insignificant. On top of this, we have thought that the remedy for our wickedness is to fight it. The more attention you give to not hearing lies and seductions the more you hear them. But the more you simply listen to the Lord the more you will turn deaf to the seductions and lies of the enemy.

It is a great mistake to give attention to your sins in order to overcome them. We couldn't be more wrong. That is the tree of the knowledge of Good and Evil. "I know what is right and I know what is wrong. I can handle this myself." So we grit our teeth and grip a cross and hope to sweat our way into holiness. In some cases we groan and cry something like, "Lord, I beg You. Help me do this or not do that!" This is not Christianity. Real Christianity is the reception of Life. It is the Tree of Life. It is dependency upon God's Life being received into us, so that Christ may live in and through us.

The first temptation in the garden was to believe that we do not need the reception of the Life that comes from God. So it is today. Religion has made her case against our desperate need of Him, or should I say enjoying His presence and voice as our one and only source of Life. But only if we will eat His fruit, will we be able to bear fruit.

CHAPTER NINE

Due Season

"There is no condition of life in which we cannot abide in Jesus. We have to learn to abide in Him wherever we are placed."

—Oswald Chambers

"At present there is too much hurry, and bustle and outward working to allow the calm working of the Spirit on my heart...but The Dew comes down when all of nature is at rest."

—Robert Murray M'Cheyne

"Only the divine nourishment will dispense the nutrients in the soul needed for the representation of His nature."

—Quote from the Author

I also love that the psalmist points out in "*due season*." This points to the beautiful principles of agriculture: time and process of the yielding fruit. There is the effortless receiving of the nutrients that, over time, effortlessly bear forth fruit.

Do not be discouraged if you don't see absolute perfection in your life right away. The goal is not so much perfection as it is being completely given over to the process by which we receive Him as our Life. Your chief responsibility is to enjoy Him, receive Him, and delight in Him, and the nutrients that are dispensed throughout your being will eventually bring about God's own nature. We need God's nourishment to give us God's nutrients that we may in time bear God's nature.

CHAPTER TEN

Will You Eat with Me?

"When an angel visited Roland Buck the angel spoke to him of a 'blackboard Christ, a diagrammed Christ, a printed Christ...' He said that Jesus wants to be known as the living Christ coming out of the pages."

(Angels on Assignment by Roland Buck)

"The testimony of Jesus is not that He gives you life but that He is the life. It is not that He gives you bread but that He is the bread"

—T. Austin Sparks

"A man is bound to his own lusts and self-centered cravings until he lies at the feet of Him who feds with bread from another world."

—Quote from the Author

Our greatest need isn't a greater resolve to not do this or that anymore, but rather to eat the Bread that Comes Down from Heaven and drink that cup of wine that comes from His hand (John 6; Matthew 26). Don't worry about your issues...simply enjoy Him and let Him cause the growth.

David in Psalm 23 gives us a glorious picture of the fact that we have been invited into a Kingdom of which Jesus said, "*is like a feast*" (Matthew 22:2). David in the valley of the shadow of death is surrounded with physical enemies who want to physically kill him with physical weapons. Yet, even in such a brutal circumstance God seems to have only one thing on His mind: "Will you eat with Me?" God isn't even concerned with these other things. He simply says, "Will you eat with Me?"

"*Thou preparest a table before me in the presence of my enemies.*" In this we learn that in any situation in life, we are not to fix our eyes on this or that, but rather, we need to fix our eyes on the fact that there is a table descending out of heaven with a tender invitation to communion with Him. We live by Him through the enjoyment of Him. We abide in Him through the enjoyment of His life.

Lastly, the original thought of this writing, *"his leaf shall not wither...."* A *"Well done, thy good and faithful servant"* is not the result of the harsh training of a spiritual Navy Seal or the rigorous intensity of a spiritual Olympian training for the great day of performance. It is rather the result of a life-long dependent and delightful feasting upon God Himself.

I wish I could impart this into every Christian heart—our greatest need is the real, living, vibrant, blinding delight in God. It will produce an endless preoccupation with Him that firmly plants us in Him. In the refreshing presence of His Spirit, where the things of value lie, we will effortlessly yield divine produce. We ourselves will be lively and revived through anything and everything that comes against us. We shall be blessed with the beauty of godly prosperity in everything we do.

CHAPTER ELEVEN

Perception of God

"Gazing…that I may indeed behold Him for whom I yearn for so long. I languish with love. Set on fire, I linger in heavenly savours. I am consumed by fire within, I recognize my beloved, the heavenly flames blaze within my soul and I do not desire anything but Him, my desire, I am entranced by divine sweetness."

—Richard Rolle

"A certain sweet gift flows in the soul and as if drunk with strong wine she melts completely into the pleasure of Him."

—Richard Rolle

"Inebriate my spirit with the burning wine of Your sweetest love, so that forgetting all evils and all limited sights, illusions and images, I may embrace You alone."

—Richard Rolle

The common question that I receive is, "Why don't I feel God?" And we have all been counseled at one time or another with the statement, "We cannot go by what we feel." Is this true? Should we be so indifferent to whether or not we "feel" God that it does not matter either way? Should we be so disconnected from "feeling" His presence that we present experience as some sort of lottery?

Charles Spurgeon once noted, "Only a corpse is without feeling" (*The Treasure of David*). Philip Krill wrote in his book, *Life in the Trinity*, "We are never without feeling." John Bunyan wrote of prayer, "Prayer is a sensible feeling in the heart" (*Prayer*). A. W. Tozer wrote, "...worship not a duty we perform but a presence we experience" (*Experiencing the Presence of God*). I believe these statements to ring true.

The question is not whether or not we should feel God, but rather what does it mean to "feel God?" The dictionary defines "feeling" as "an emotional state or reaction." Looking into the life of Jesus we see that He did nothing apart from the empowerment of spiritual perception of His Father. Perception is defined as, "the ability to see, or hear or sense." The sense of God is not just important; it is our source of spiritual empowerment. Our spiritual "feeling" as stated in the Scriptures, is simply, *"joy unspeakable and full of glory."* First Peter 1:8,

> *"Whom having not seen, ye love; in whom through now ye see him not, yet believing, ye rejoice with joy unspeakable and full of glory."*

Yes, this is our portion under His rule. Even though we don't physically see Him, we experience Him, in joy and glory. We don't see Him, but we perceive Him. Moses endured, "seeing Him who is unseen." The early Christian writers spoke of the "imageless vision."

Feeling rightly defined as spiritual perceptibility in the Scriptures simply means that *"peace that passes all understanding"* is the Life source and guidance of those whose minds and hearts are stayed upon Him.

> *"And the peace of God, which passes all understanding, shall keep your hearts and minds through Christ Jesus."*

Peace enjoyed and beyond comprehension. What does this mean? Well, maybe it could be better seen as this, "It makes absolutely no sense to have peace right now, but I do." Such wonderful peace acts as a guard for your mind and your heart. God's protection over your heart and mind is the experience of His presence that blissfully numbs our souls to doubt, fear, reason, questions, etc. Our only job is to look at Him. Isaiah 26:3:

> *"You will keep him in perfect peace whose mind is stayed on You."*

In the Scriptures, feeling simply means that the rule of the great King established in our souls is not a matter of what we talk about but rather peace and joy in the presence of God who is the Holy Spirit. Romans 14:17:

> *"For the Kingdom of God is not meat and drink; but righteousness, and peace, and joy in the Holy Ghost."*

Rest is the realm of perception and reception of God. God has promised us that when we are under His shadow, joy and peace and comfort and grace and empowerment are not only ours but are our Life supply. Read these next two sentences slowly.

Jesus is the only person who is all at once.
The Bliss of His realm is what He in fact is.

When we speak of feelings we are not speaking of physical sensation but rather internal perceptibility. Yet, at the same time Thomas Dubay once wrote, "We are so one that the interinfluence between spiritual and material elements is unavoidable" (*Fire Within*). There are many times that our bodies experience the overflow of the glorious inflow of God. David writes in Psalm 23 that his cup was so full to the brim that it overflowed to the outside of the cup. The external feelings are not what is promised. What is promised to us is the experience of God's person when we come to Him. Rest itself is a promised feeling and work of the Lamb of God who said in Matthew 11:28,

"Come to me and I will give you rest."

Satisfaction is itself a promised feeling. Jesus said in John 7:37,

"...if any man is thirsty let him come to Me and drink."

Being fed in our spirit is a feeling we can feel, and Jesus said that He would feed those who hunger (see John 6).

Feeling is inseparable from experience. Experience is inseparable from feeling. People ask me if I experience God every time that I pray. My answer is always the same. Yes, because without experience it is simply not communion with a person.

A. W. Tozer once wrote, "The tragedy of the church is that from childhood to old age men have only known a synthetic God compounded of theology and logic; having no eyes to see and no ears to hear" (*Evenings With Tozer*). The terrible indictment against the church is that we have substituted logic for Life. Jesus condemned the Pharisees not because of their lack of knowing God's words but because they had no idea what God was saying and no living experience of God's person.

Feeling God, experiencing God, is not an option or perk of His presence. It is rather the means by which He frees us and empowers us to be able to obey Him. The experience of God is the enjoyment of the New Covenant, the Covenant in which God Himself would make His abode in us. John 14:23:

> *"If a man love me, he will keep my words; and my Father will love him, and we will come unto him, and make our abode with him."*

The Covenant in which God would put His Spirit on the inside of us. First Corinthians 2:12:

"We have received...the Spirit which is of God."

The Covenant that is spoken of as new wine. The Covenant in which our fellowship is with Jesus Christ the Son. The Covenant in which seeing and hearing, experiencing, and yes, even sensing the Glorious Word of Life within is our lot, our source, and our strength. Jesus refused to act outside of the empowerment of spiritually perceiving His Father, saying, "The Son can do nothing of Himself. He can only do what He sees His Father doing...." Because He is the Son and the only prototype man, He reveals to us that a son can do nothing of himself. This is the reason why religion hates sonship. Jesus was calling God His own Father and they had not been born of God.

None of Jesus' works had their origin in Himself, but all of their works issued out of themselves. Jesus is showing us that sonship has its roots in the great love with which the Father has loved us in giving to us His own Spirit, and that walking out sonship is living in synchronization with God through spiritual perception of God.

CHAPTER TWELVE

Communion Is Imperative

"When you are quiet before God, simply allow yourself time to enjoy His presence and be filled full in your spirit...hearing is a passive rather than an active procedure. Rest. Rest. Rest in God's love. Simply listen and be attentive to God. These passive actions will permit God to communicate His love to you.... When your spirit is centered on God all activities He initiates will be full of peace and natural and so spontaneous that it will appear to you that there has hardly been any activity at all."

— Madame Guyon
(*Experiencing the Depths of Jesus Christ*)

When you turn and sustain your gaze whole-heartedly in adoration upon God, little by little your soul will begin to detach from the cares of this world. It will release your heart from self-consciousness and dissolve the "itch of efforts."

At this point, His presence will begin to manifest. By this I mean a sense of sweet tranquility that moves throughout your being, as a direct result of the soul yielding to the Spirit. We must note that in that moment the purpose of prayer is being accomplished. Here we resign ourselves to linger, content with Him alone. Then as we linger, gazing upon Him by sustaining all of our attention upon Him, we will be able to hear His voice, experience His heart, and see His speaking through various means, the richest of which is in meditation upon the Scriptures that He illuminates.

This is very simple but herein lies the issue: men cannot hear God, experience His heart, nor can they see His speaking, simply because their hearts are not giving attention to His presence. The sad fact is that, His presence is no longer the purpose of prayer for many people. Most people don't even think this way. In most cases His presence has been eclipsed by external rituals, things to do, and efforts to make themselves feel productive.

We must recognize that if someone is trying to lead us or communicate to us, our attention is paramount. If our attention is not fully given to the leader or communicator by listening, by looking, and by concentration, their attempt to communicate to us will not be received in wholeness because we are divided in our attention, in our listening, and in our looking.

Our relationship with God hinges upon our attentiveness and wholehearted fixation upon His person and presence. No matter how subtle it may seem in the moment or how meaningless, it is in our looking and in our listening that we find the very source Himself. The subtle impressions will increase into ecstatic blissful currents if we choose to remain yielded. This is what is needed to obtain the blissful currents of God that are needed to make us more like Him.

This bliss will numb the soul to unbelief, questions, the itch to do, the craving to be noticed, the lusts of the soul, and even the body's longings. Such experiential communion brings us into the experience of our individual union with God that Christ has given to us.

Union. Here is life's greatest joy, peace, satisfaction, success, and pleasure, whether we preach to millions or change tires, whether our name is known or never heard in this life. No one pleases God and carries the Kingdom of God into the earth like a man united with God, living in a life of intimate communion.

Maxims

His hands are outstretched, waiting to melt or hearts with His tender touch. We just need to sit down and quietly give our souls up to Him.

There may come moments throughout your day when you don't sense His presence, but there's never a time when you cannot sense His presence.

Christianity is not a relationship with our own commitment. It is, rather, the enjoyment of the living Christ through surrender to His rule.

"Apart from me you can do nothing" simply means without His presence we are utterly helpless.

The phrase, "Cease striving and know the I Am," is a command to replace efforts with communion.

There are many things that will be established through His presents, but without His presence nothing can be established.

The best way to let people know that He is alive today is to let them see you reflecting His life as He lives in you.

— Roland Buck

God's tenderheartedness towards you is so great that His receiving you when you come to Him is an absolute certainty.

❦

I am so sick of the moments throughout my day that I get distracted from yielding into the blissful empowerment of His presence.

❦

If the presence of Jesus isn't the center, then Jesus is not the center.

❦

The heart that aches for Jesus is evidence that the Spirit has printed the first commandment upon the soul.

❦

Those that do not enjoy the Lord are not free to be led by Him, because they are still bound to things they want from Him.

❦

A man is bound to his own lusts and self-centered cravings until he lies at the feet of Him who feeds with bread from another world.

Beware of being dependent upon your own resolve, because a son can do nothing of himself.

So often, our desires for other things sabotage our ability to be led by the Spirit.

Here is our job: To stare at the Lamb of God and from that place, to call out to everyone to do the same.

There is an effortless fruit that comes out of a man when the enjoyment of Christ is inside of that man.

Only the bliss of sustained, still adoration can plunge deep enough to suffocate the constant rise of self and rebellion in the soul.

✑

If we get still and adore Him, we will perceive Him. If we will give attention to that perception, we will pass through it into Him.

✑

"I don't believe in spiritual sensations," said the Christian.

✑

The old prophet smiled. "You will, when you see Him."

✑

Ezekiel begins with the glory of God and ends with the building of a house. This is what the glory does; He builds His house.

✑

Humility is not gained by principles or by practices but rather time in God's presence.

❧

How do I hear God? Let Him hold you.

❧

There is an irreplaceable work that the bliss of His presence works in the soul. We are daily in need of it.

❧

Worry is the most common sign of distrust in God.

❧

Sit quiet and still. Hold your heart on Him in adoration, nothing more or less, for as long as you can. Again and again.

❧

Nothing will heighten your ability to sense His presence like daily blocking out time to simply cling to Him in adoration.

MAXIMS

⚮

We come to know Him by His presence. No presence, no knowing.

⚮

Begin at the beginning. Be faithful in the inner chamber...Bow in silence before the Lord, who so longs for you.

— Andrew Murray

⚮

Have we forgotten that getting quiet before God is our strength?

⚮

Rest is not the ceasing of all activity but His presence as the source and power of all our activity.

⚮

Oh that we would understand that God is far more interested in lovers than Olympians.

From the household you can judge what the parents are: the parents make it what it is. The household is the outgrowth and the expression of the parents' lives.

— Andrew Murray

Striving is evidence of a feeble knowledge of God.

If I cling to His presence, then I will always know where He is, and I will always be where I'm supposed to be.

He died that you might enjoy Him, and through enjoying Him you would be conformed to His image, and by His image accomplish His purposes.

Wisdom in life from Solomon:
1. Don't talk about other people.
2. Avoid drama.
3. Be someone others can trust.

— Proverbs 20:3, 6, 19

Religion is seeking God without spiritual perception of God.

"In the beginning was the Word" shows us that every divine work starts with God's speaking.

Only if He is everything can He safely give us anything.

Lord, in Your sweet presence I become aware of how I am constantly forgetting how wonderful You really are.

If our heart stops aching for Jesus, we are out of sync with God.

∽

There is a learning that only comes from leaning.

∽

There is no remedy for a man who will not come away.

∽

Refusing to sin is far inferior to refusing to depart.

∽

Only if His presence is the center of our lives can His presence actually be the source of our lives.

∽

How can we say we fear Him if we will not wait for Him?

❧

Why does God raise up all who are bowed down? Because being bowed down means losing all concerned with ever being raised up at all.

❧

We must learn to behold His beauty and inhale Him that we may express Him.

— Witness Lee

❧

When time in the presence of the Lord is number one...we become very selective as to what things we allow in our day.

❧

Holiness is much more than separation; it is fellowship and enjoyment of God.

— Andrew Murray

❧

Three downfalls of pride:
1. Loss of spiritual life
2. Absence of love
3. Inability to learn

— Michael Dow

Jesus frequently and emphatically alluded to His personal connection with the Father as the means by which He lived.

— Andrew Murray

Abiding in Christ means refusing to let anything distract you from the sweet empowering presence of God.

Enjoyment of God is the purest form of seeking God.

Some of us want to be instantaneously delivered from everything so that we will not have to actually cling to Jesus moment by moment.

※

To not wait for His voice is to forfeit the Divine Shielding.

※

The itch to do something in prayer stems from a desire for something more than just Him.

※

The presence of the Spirit will quicken our minds, our affections, and most importantly our wills to be aligned with His. Simply come to Him.

※

In fellowship with God, sin is powerless.
— Andrew Murray

※

Dependency is maturing when we realize that even our resolve is worthless.

∽

"...dependence in continual waiting on the Father was the root of Christ's implicit obedience...."
— Andrew Murray

∽

It is only when the commands come from the Living Voice that obedience will be possible and acceptable.
— Andrew Murray

∽

"However full and blessed the past experience may be, its power depends upon the fresh inflow of the divine life...."
— Jessie Penn-Lewis

∽

Seduction thrives where delight is lacking.

✿

"Her very helplessness is her safety."
— Jessie Penn-Lewis on The Bride

✿

Outward likeness can only be the manifestation of a living inward union.
— Andrew Murray

✿

The Spirit's special work is to maintain the fellowship of God with men.

✿

Jonathan wasn't selfishly interested in wearing the crown, but rather selflessly interested in it being on the right head.

✿

The godly man is "unimpressive" simply because his godliness is so natural and true that he never comes off as some celestial being.

Authentic godliness is when we enjoy the Lord before or even without the answer to our requests.

About the Author

Eric and Brooke Gilmour

Sonship International is a ministry started by Eric and Brooke Gilmour, seeking to bring the church into a deeper experience of God in their daily lives while preaching the Gospel throughout the world. Graduate of the Brownsville Revival School of Ministry, Eric conducts The School of His Presence in the United States and abroad. Eric is a conference speaker and author of the books *Burn, Union, Into the Cloud, Divine Life, Enjoying the Gospel,* and *The School of His Presence,* and *Nostalgia.*

Notes

NOTES

_____
_____
_____
_____
_____
_____
_____
_____
_____
_____
_____
_____
_____
_____
_____
_____
_____
_____
_____
_____
_____
_____
_____
_____
_____
_____
_____
_____
_____
_____

NOTES

_____
_____
_____
_____
_____
_____
_____
_____
_____
_____
_____
_____
_____
_____
_____
_____
_____
_____
_____
_____
_____
_____
_____
_____
_____
_____

NOTES

_____

_____

_____

_____

_____

_____

_____

_____

_____

_____

_____

_____

_____

_____

_____

_____

_____

_____

_____

_____

_____

_____

_____

_____

Bibliography

A'Kempis, Thomas. *Imitation of Christ*. Catholic Book Publishing Corporation, 2015.

Buck, Roland. *Angels on Assignment*. Whitaker House, 2005.

Chambers, Oswald. *My Utmost for His Highest*. Discovery House, 2016.

Fee, Gordon. *God's Empowering Presence*. Hendrickson.

Gilmour, James. *His Diaries, Letters and Reports*. Forgotten Books, 2012.

Guyon, Madame. *A Short and Easy Method of Prayer*. CreateSpace Independent Publishing Platform, 2015.

Guyon, Madame. *Experiencing the Depths of Jesus Christ*. Christian Books Pub House, 1981.

Lee, Witness. *Life-Study of John*. Living Stream Ministry, 1985.

Lee, Witness. *The Wonderful Being of Christ*. Living Stream Ministry, 1983.

M'Cheyne, Robert Murray. *Memoirs and Remains of the Rev. Robert Mccheyne*. Forgotten Books, 2012.

McGinn, Bernard. *The Essential Writings of Christian Mysticism*. Modern Library, 2006.

Murray, Andrew. *The Prayer Life*. Rough Draft Printing, 2014.

Penn-Lewis, Jessie. *Thy Hidden Ones*. CLC Publications, 1995.

Rolle, Richard. *Richard Rolle: The English Writings*. Paulist Press.

St. Teresa of Avila. *Interior Castle*. Dover Publications, 2007.

Schlink, Mother Basilea. *My All for Him*. Bethany House Publishers, 2000.

BIBLIOGRAPHY

Sparks, T. Austin. *We Beheld His Glory*. Book Ministry, 2012.

Stanley, Charles. *How to Listen to God*. Thomas Nelson, 2002.

Taylor, Jeremy. *Holy Living*.

Tozer, A. W. *Experiencing God*. Regal Books.

Tozer, A. W. *The Pursuit of God*. CreateSpace Independent Publishing Platform, 2016.

Additional Books
by Eric Gilmour

Burn: Melting into the Image of Jesus

Union: The Thirsting Soul Satisfied in God

Into the Cloud: Becoming God's Spokesman

Enjoying the Gospel

Divine Life: Conversations on the Spiritual Life

The School of His Presence

Nostalgia

Available on:

Amazon, Nook, Kindle, Kobo, iBooks

BURN

God is raising up mystical wonder workers who seek oneness with God through surrender and bleed deliverance to this sin sick world. In this book lies the pillars to becoming the Jesus people in the earth today — hose who manifest the Person of Christ through character, power and wisdom.

UNION

"If you come to Him for something other than Him, you will miss Him."

"Men are bent against pleasure in the Spirit to the degree that they don't experience it."

The Christian life that isn't satisfied with God alone, testifies to the world that God isn't enough."

"Part of the reason most Christians are not eager to give people what they have, is because what they have doesn't satisfy them."

In *Union*, Eric W. Gilmour explains the relationship God desires to have with every believer. It is up to you to initiate your part in His planned "Union" with Him.

INTO THE CLOUD

"The prophet has become his message. He does not prepare messages, he speaks what has been spoken into him; he speaks what has been spoken into him; he speaks what he himself has become."

"Obedience is when a man's life is yielded to the extent that God can perform through that man the things He has spoken to him." "We must seek to find Christ present in the depths of the scriptures, not merely as type and shadow, but as the living word, the present speaking of God."

ENJOYING THE GOSPEL

The gospel is the offering of God's presence to men. It is the invitation into a life of experiencing Him. The inspiration of our lives must be our past experiences of Him; our satisfaction must be our present experience of Him; 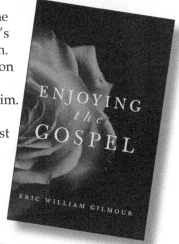 our hunger is for our future experiences of Him. I would much rather touch Him than attempt to define Him. I would rather move Him than seek to simply understand Him. I would rather know Him than merely perform His works.

Are you with me?

Let us live our lives enjoying this glorious gospel!

DIVINE LIFE

This book has been compiled from conversations on the Spiritual Life between Eric Gilmour, Michael Dow and David Popovici.

NOSTALGIA: GOD'S BROKEN HEART

God's heart is broken as His people look to other things for satisfaction, joy and peace. He is not willing to let them go. He relays His anguish through Hosea, the broken-hearted

prophet. In this prophetic book lies the core speaking of God to the Western world. Wrought with divine nostalgia, God calls His people to solitude with Him that He may whisper into their ears and be their deliverance and all satisfying lover. Though others cried, "injustice" Hosea cries, "You don't love me anymore."

Made in United States
North Haven, CT
20 July 2023

39309528R00082